THIS BOOK BELONGS TO:

....

(the 'Superstar Cat')

AND

....

(the 'Facilitating Human')

SUPERSTAR CATS

**Easy tricks that will give your cat
the spotlight they deserve**

Julie Tottman

SEVEN DIALS

First published in Great Britain in 2017 by Seven Dials
An imprint of Orion Publishing Group Ltd
Carmelite House, 50 Victoria Embankment, London, EC4Y 0DZ

An Hachette UK Company

10 9 8 7 6 5 4 3 2 1

Text © Julie Tottman 2017

The right of Julie Tottman to be identified as the author of this work has been
asserted in accordance with the Copyright, Designs and Patents Act 1988.

A CIP catalogue record for this book is available
from the British Library.

ISBN: 9781409174905

Cover photography: Shutterstock
Illustrations: Emanuel Santos

Printed and bound by CPI Group (UK) Ltd, Croydon, CR0 4YY

The Orion Publishing Group's policy is to use papers that are natural,
renewable and recyclable products and made from wood grown in
sustainable forests. The logging and manufacturing processes are expected
to conform to the environmental regulations of the country of origin.

Every effort has been made to ensure that the information in this book is
accurate. The information in this book may not be applicable or suitable
for every cat. People should check for themselves if their animal is able to
perform the tricks and also to ensure their own safety. If you are concerned
about the health of your pet or its ability to perform any of the actions in
the book, you should consult a veterinarian practitioner first. Neither the
publisher nor author accepts any responsibility for any personal injury or
other damage or loss arising from the use of the information in this book.

MIX
Paper from
responsible sources
FSC® C104740
FSC
www.fsc.org

www.orionbooks.co.uk

CONTENTS

HELLO FELLOW CAT LOVER!

I've filled this book with tricks I've been teaching cat 'actors' for the last two decades; some cute, some funny, but all impressive. All the tricks here can be taught by anyone, ranging from the easy – such as teaching your cat to rub (page 86) – to ones which require a little more patience and practice – such as 'Bring an object' (page 107). All of them are worth the effort!

Something I'm often asked is if cats are too free-spirited to be trained. Well, there are certainly some who prefer to be trained more than others (see page 19), but I can tell you I've trained cats for a whole bunch of films and adverts. From *Harry Potter* and *Skyfall* to *Angus, Thongs and Perfect Snogging*, I've had cats stretching, waving, jumping up and even massaging!

In my experience, the majority of cats are very trainable – but in order for it to work your cat needs to be domesticated, like being petted and be very motivated by treats. So long as they're friendly and playful, and you as their trainer have enthusiasm, rewards and patience in abundance, then I promise he or she can be rivalling the movie stars in no time – and you'll be building a beautiful bond with your cat whilst you're at it. Good luck!

A BIT ABOUT ME

I've been an animal trainer for film and television for over twenty years, something I still pinch myself about. Animals have always been my absolute passion; at 13 I started working in a poodle parlour on Saturdays and I did my apprenticeship there when I left school, becoming a doggy hairdresser soon after. It hadn't crossed my mind to look into animal training as a career until a friend's father – an art director in the film industry – told me the job existed. I couldn't believe it: getting paid to play with animals all day and go on film sets? It was too good to be true.

I felt sure I didn't stand a chance of breaking into it, but I managed to find the names of some agencies through a friend in the industry and I eagerly contacted all of them. I did a lot of work for free before I finally landed a full-time job, and a few years later I was given an amazing opportunity when I was asked to work for an internationally acclaimed training company, Birds and Animals. I've now run the UK branch for 18 years.

One of the things I love about my job is how different each day is. At any one time, I might be working on anything between one and eight feature films, as well as adverts and TV shows, and over the years I've trained reindeer, monkeys, mongoose and bats, to name just a few. But, after dogs, cats are the animal I'm asked to train most often – not surprising, as they are one of the most popular pets in the world. (Fish are the most popular – but luckily I've never been asked to train them!)

I love cats, but they can be stubborn little so-and-sos: they're all clever enough to be trained but it takes the right sort of nature to get success – just like humans, not all cats want to be actors. This means casting the right cat is very important. The main thing I look for is confidence. Some cats get very stressed by being moved around, which is really unfair for them, so I'm always on the lookout for brave cats who I know will enjoy the limelight. The second thing I look for is greediness! I'm always after a cat who likes to be petted and picked up, but if they're really motivated by treats then that makes trick training much easier.

I try to rescue as many animals as I can when it comes to casting. Once I have the description of the particular type of animal needed, I contact rescue centres to see if they have any that fit the bill and are in need of a home. My favourite cat I've cast was Crookshanks for the Harry Potter series. The casting team wanted a grumpy-looking cat, so I straight away thought of a Persian as I love them; they have such characterful faces. I found the perfect candidate – a cat called Crackerjack who was just the best cat to work with; he'd trot along beside me almost like a dog. We were real partners for many years, and he carried on living with me after the films ended. I sadly lost him to old age in 2016, but I still have Max, who played Mrs Norris!

HOW TO USE THIS BOOK

Hopefully you've bought (or been given) this book because you already have a cat; so long as you have one, the rest is very simple!

☐ Have a read of 'Top tips for success' (page xx), which offers lots of advice on how to get started and teach tricks successfully.

☐ Start with the tricks in 'The Essentials' chapter – your cat needs to know these before you move on to any others.

☐ Before you begin each trick, take a look at the key at the top for the following information:

🕐 the average length of time it will take for your cat to be performing the trick perfectly on cue.

what you'll need to successfully teach the trick.

 the tricks your cat needs to know already before you attempt the trick you're looking at.

Each time you finish a trick, sign the box at the bottom of the page. Then, when your cat has successfully completed all the tricks in the book, award him or her the coveted certificate at the very back and let your cat do a smug lap of honour around your sitting room.

TOP TIPS FOR SUCCESS

The below FAQs provide some useful advice on how to approach trick training and give you and your cat the best chance of success. Give them a read-through before you get stuck into the tricks.

Q: WHERE IS THE BEST PLACE TO TEACH MY CAT TRICKS?

A: It's important to do your sessions somewhere your cat is very familiar with. Make sure it's quiet and that there's nothing to distract your cat whilst you are training together.

Q: WHEN IS THE BEST TIME TO TEACH MY CAT A TRICK?

A: Before a meal – that way they will be much more motivated by the treat reward. When cats are full all they want to think about is sleeping – quite right too!

Q: HOW LONG SHOULD THE TRAINING SESSIONS BE?

A: Cats generally need shorter training sessions than dogs as they can get frustrated quickly if they don't understand what you are asking for (and they're generally much more free-spirited!). Practise little and often, instead of doing long, frustrating training sessions. I'd recommend bursts of 15–20 minutes and no more than four sessions a day.

Q: HOW MANY TRICKS CAN I TEACH MY CAT AT ONCE?
A: Keep it to about three tricks at any one time. This will also keep your sessions more focused.

Q: HOW SHOULD I PRAISE MY CAT? HOW MUCH FUSS SHOULD I MAKE?
A: By saying 'good' (or 'good boy'/'good girl') in a positive, animated way – the tone of your voice is key here. You can pet them as well – most cats enjoy the treat more than the fuss, but keep both going throughout. You can make less of a song and dance about it once they are doing it consistently, but never stop praising or giving them a treat altogether. Reassure your cat all the time during training. Never, ever scold your cat – trick training is all about the carrot, never the stick!

Q: HOW DO I GIVE MY CAT THE TREAT?

A: I recommend you place the treat in a little cat bowl and feed the reward from this – cats have very sharp claws and teeth so they can hurt you by accident when being enthusiastic about the reward, so don't do it from your hand. The bowl then starts acting as a prompt – when they see the bowl they understand training time is coming. Mine will start to rub around my legs or jump up to try to steal the treats from the magic bowl!

Q: WHERE SHOULD I KEEP MY TREATS?

A: Close by so you can pop one in your treat bowl whenever you need one.

Q: WHEN I'M REWARDING MY CAT, DOES IT MATTER WHICH WAY ROUND I SAY 'GOOD' AND GIVE THE TREAT?

A: You should tell them 'good' as soon as they have done the task requested and whilst you are going in to give them the treat from the bowl.

Q: WHAT TREATS SHOULD I USE?

A: This is very much dependent on what your cat likes and you may need to experiment with different types to find the right one for your cat. Some like commercial treats, whereas other prefer little bits of fish or meat. It's very important, however, to make sure your cat doesn't become overweight and have too much salt or fat in their diet. If you are doing lots of sessions, be aware of how much you are feeding throughout the day and alter their main meal accordingly.

Q: IS THERE A TIME WHEN I CAN ASK MY CAT TO DO A TRICK WITHOUT GIVING A REWARD AT THE END OF IT?

A: You should always reward your cat, even for the simplest task. Once they have learnt several tricks you can ask for them in a row and then reward at the end. I also like to keep rewarding for the basic behaviours (such as sit and stay), as if these get weak it has a knock-on effect for other tricks.

Q: WHAT MOOD SHOULD MY CAT BE IN FOR THE BEST CHANCE OF SUCCESS?

A: Like us, cats tend to be lethargic if it's really hot, so wait until it's cool before you begin. Also, if they are sleepy or full they won't want to learn – so let them have a rest and do a training session later.

Q: ARE THERE CERTAIN TYPES OF CATS THAT ARE EASIER TO TRAIN THAN OTHERS?

A: It's mainly about personality: the ideal cat to train is friendly, playful and likes treats, as they are the main motivator for cats. In general, though, I'd say Maine Coons, Siamese and Bengals are great. Persians are smart but a little lazier than the feistier breeds.

Q: HOW DO I LET MY CAT KNOW THAT THE TRICK IS OVER?

A: I generally give them a cuddle to say they have done well and indicate that the session is over.

FIVE FINAL TOP TIPS . . .

1 LITTLE AND OFTEN. It is much better to do four short sessions a day than one long one. Your cat will become bored if you make it too long. Keep it fun.

2 PRAISE, PRAISE, TREATS. Trick training is all about encouragement but it's also about rewards – make sure you are giving your cat what they are motivated by each time they perform a trick correctly.

3 NEVER GET CROSS! Quite often if my cat isn't doing something right, it'll be because I'm doing something wrong. If your cat isn't understanding a command, re-read the instructions and start again another day. NEVER yell at or smack your cat. If he or she is having a cheeky day and misbehaving, simply stop the training and ignore the naughty behaviour. This will really make him or her want to be a good boy or girl, next time, as they will feel they've missed out on fun times!

4 BE CONSISTENT. Just like humans, cats respond well to routines. Aim to keep where, when and how long your trick training sessions are consistent, as well as how you ask for a trick to be performed and how you praise a good performance. As said above, it's crucial you always keep the place you are training your cat safe and secure – you don't want your cat to be scared and run off.

5 END ON A HIGH. Where possible, finish on a good note when your cat has achieved the behaviour or is getting close.

THE ESSENTIALS

The following basic behaviours form the
basis of most other tricks you'll want to teach
your cat, so it's worth making sure she or he is
comfortable with doing all these first.
Once you're both happily doing these
then the sky's the limit!

SIT

2–3 DAYS

TASTY TREATS AND TREAT BOWL

—

This is a basic trick that is essential for your cat to know and is fairly easy to teach. Most cats pick it up quite quickly with repeat practice over 2–3 days – I'd say try doing it about 4 times a day. Little and often is key to ensure your cat always enjoys himself but remembers what it is that's being asked of him.

HOW TO START

Have your cat in front of you on the floor. Kneel in front of him and make sure he knows you have a treat.

HOW TO DO

- Bring the treat up over your cat's head and then slightly behind him, so that he has to look up. As a result, he will put his bottom down – as he does this say '**sit**'. If he does it then praise him and reward him straight away.

- Keep practising to make sure he understands the **sit** cue – put your hand gently underneath his tummy to lift him up, then repeat the trick. Once your cat understands, you can just use the cue and will not need to raise the treat above his head.

TIP

If your cat doesn't sit then do not put your hand on his bottom to help ease it down, as people sometimes do with dogs – this has the opposite effect on cats and he will lift his bottom higher! Instead, reward any lowering of his bottom, even if it doesn't touch the ground, and keep repeating – his bottom should get lower and lower each time you do it.

I STARTED THIS TRICK ON: ....

I COMPLETED THIS TRICK BY: ....

GO TO MARK

2–3 DAYS **TASTY TREATS AND TREAT BOWL, BLOCK OF WOOD/BIG, HEAVY BOOK** **—**

The object of this is to be able to send or call your cat to a particular point, or a 'mark', as it's called in animal training. I've used this trick in pretty much every film I've ever worked on, but my favourite memory was for a cat litter advert where I had to get one cat to massage another! The cat in question was called Frisco, and I used this trick (and 'Pad', see page 73) to get him to do it.

HOW TO START

You'll need an object to act as the 'mark'; something which is big enough for your cat's front feet to comfortably fit on, and which is just high enough for her to have to make a step up onto, so she realises there is a difference between the mark and the ground. I'd suggest a sturdy block of wood or a big solid book. Place or lead your cat just in front of the mark.

HOW TO DO

- Pop a treat in the treat bowl and then use this to lure your cat forward so that her feet step onto the mark. As she does this, say '**mark**'. As soon as her feet touch the mark (even if it is just one foot in the beginning) praise her and give her the reward immediately.

- Repeat until you feel confident that she understands what is being asked of her.

- Then, instead of placing her in front of the mark and luring her forward with the treat, you can stand behind the mark and give her the cue. If she struggles with this then go back to guiding her – always remember that patience is key with cat training.

- Once your cat knows the trick well, you can advance it by building the distance between you, and making the mark smaller and flatter.

TIP

Repetition is the key to this! Keeping your cat standing on the mark whilst praising her is helpful, along with giving her plenty of treats for staying there.

If your cat won't step on the mark, make it bigger so there's no chance she can miss it. If she's really struggling, you can gently lift her paws up onto the mark, but try to avoid this if you can as you'll have much more success rewarding her for making the choice to do it herself.

I STARTED THIS TRICK ON: ....

I COMPLETED THIS TRICK BY: ....

STAY

2–3 DAYS

TASTY TREATS AND TREAT BOWL, BLOCK OF WOOD/BIG, HEAVY BOOK

SIT, GO TO MARK

Teaching your cat to stay in one place is a basic trick that paves the way for lots of others – you're never going to get very far if your cat is running off every time you're asking him to do something! The easiest way for your cat to learn this one is if he's already mastered 'sit' or 'go to mark', so that you can ask him to stay in one of those positions.

HOW TO START

Ask your cat to sit or mark – whichever one he feels more confident doing. Stand in front of him with a treat in your hand.

HOW TO DO

- Make sure your cat knows you have a treat and use this to keep his focus on you.

- Then tell him to '**stay**' whilst holding the palm of your hand up in front of you, the way a lollipop lady might to stop traffic. If your cat stays for a second without fidgeting then tell him 'good' and reward him with the treat. If your cat gets up and tries to come towards you then gently carry him back to the start and try again. If he walks away without interest then it is important that you don't try to force him to stay, as this could result in him becoming agitated – just try again another day.

- Once your cat stays for one second, start building the time up very gradually, a few seconds at a time, so you don't lose your cat's interest or focus. Once he is happy to stay for about ten seconds at the original distance between you, you can start increasing the distance between you very slowly, returning to only asking him to stay for a second or so before you praise and reward him. Aim to end up with a good 2-minute stay at a distance of about 10 feet/3 metres.

TIP

Don't ask for too much from your cat too soon; the key here really is to build up time and distance slowly. Always reward your cat in the place and position you asked him to stay in to avoid confusion.

I STARTED THIS TRICK ON: ....

I COMPLETED THIS TRICK BY: ....

COME

2–3 WEEKS   **TASTY TREATS AND TREAT**   **—**
                   BOWL, TREAT TIN

This is less of a trick to show off to your friends and more of a really useful one to know for when you either want your cat to come to you for session time – or if it's firework night and you need to get her in from the garden quickly! We use this a lot on film sets, but instead of using a treat tin we use a buzzing sound from a remote buzzer.

HOW TO START

I start by standing close to the cat and shaking her
favourite treat tin, or I tap on the side of the food can.
Keep making the noise as you give her a treat so that she
associates the noise with tasty food! (The noise is the cue
here, so make sure you are always making the same noise.)

HOW TO DO

- Once she is coming nicely to the sound from a close
  distance, start to do it further away – in the next room,
  for example. I do it at intervals throughout the day
  around the house. As soon as you make the sound,
  your cat should appear (if she doesn't then you need to
  go back to step one).

- If you have a garden, you can then move your cat
  outside whilst you stand in the doorway – so she
  understands that wherever she is, as soon as that
  sound is heard a tasty snack is coming her way.

I STARTED THIS TRICK ON: ....

I COMPLETED THIS TRICK BY: ....

THE TRICKS

Now your cat is happily sitting, staying, coming and going, together you can head for the bright lights of superstardom! Stock up on those tasty treats and brush up on your enthusiastic 'good boy's and 'good girl's – it's trick time.

ON FEET

3–5 WEEKS

TASTY TREATS AND
TREAT BOWL

SIT

This is for when you want your cat to get up from a sitting position. In films, we use it when we want the cat to look alert, or to go into another trick. It's quite easy to teach as it plays on cats' instinctive reflexes, but as with all these tricks it does require a bit of practice to make sure your cat properly understands what is being asked of him.

HOW TO START

Ask your cat to sit. Kneel in front of him with a treat.

HOW TO DO

- Get your cat to focus on the treat in your hand, then gently touch just in front of his tail, on his back, whilst saying '**on your feet**'. As soon as his bottom pops up – this is a natural reaction in cats – then tell him good and reward him.

- Repeat the process over the course of about 8–10 training sessions until you feel sure your cat understands what is being asked of him, rather than it just being a reflex action. When you feel confident he's got it, then try to move on from touching his back to just the verbal cue.

I STARTED THIS TRICK ON: ....
I COMPLETED THIS TRICK BY: ....

LIE DOWN

2–4 WEEKS   **TASTY TREATS AND TREAT BOWL**   **SIT**

This is a very useful trick, and one that's easy to teach – mainly because cats love to lie down! It crops up in lots of films and adverts, but one memory in particular stands out: getting a white chinchilla Persian called Trojan to do it in Daniel Craig's lap for Spectre. Being responsible for a Bond film cat has to be a career highlight!

HOW TO START

Have a treat in your hand. Kneel in front of your cat and ask her to sit.

HOW TO DO

- Show your cat the treat and use it to keep her focus. Then, keeping the treat just out of reach, move the treat to the floor whilst saying '**down**'. If your cat makes a downward motion, praise and reward immediately – remember that a good friendly cat enjoys a stroke as a reward too!

- Repeat the process until your cat is performing the trick confidently – then you can just use **down** rather than using the treat as a lure.

TIP

If your cat doesn't go down but instead goes to move forwards, immediately bring the treat up and wait until she is back in the settled sit position and try again. Eventually she will realise that the aim is not to go forwards but to lie down.

WALK SIDEWAYS

4–6 WEEKS

TASTY TREATS AND TREAT
BOWL, DESK

—

*This is a little advanced and takes some patience,
but it's a really fun trick to get your cat to do –
people are always impressed by it!*

HOW TO START

You need a surface that's off the ground (so your cat can't walk forwards), such as a desk or a coffee table. Have a treat handy and place your cat at the front of the desk, facing you.

HOW TO DO

- Get your cat to focus on the treat, then move it sideways so that you're luring him to the side. Use the flat of your other hand to very gently coax his body towards the hand with the treat in, whilst saying '**sideways**'. If he moves to cross his legs or makes any move to walk sideways – praise and reward him immediately. Repeat and repeat and repeat. Once you feel he is starting to understand what is expected of him then you can hold your hand near to the flat of his body rather than pushing him, which will assist your verbal cue.

I STARTED THIS TRICK ON: ....

I COMPLETED THIS TRICK BY: ....

SEARCH

2–4 WEEKS

TASTY TREATS AND TREAT BOWL, WHISTLE OR EQUIVALENT

—

This is a brilliant, nice and easy trick which involves your cat searching for a noise – so once your cat is performing it confidently, kids can use it to play hide and seek (or, of course, you can!). In the film industry, where a trainer blowing a whistle would be too visible, we often make the noise using a remote control.

HOW TO START

To teach your cat to find something you need to pair a noise with a food reward. This can be any noise that won't alarm your cat – let's say a whistle for now. Again, the noise itself is the cue.

HOW TO DO

- With your cat in front of you, blow the whistle and feed her a reward straight away. After a few times of doing this, she will see the sound as a sort of dinner bell.

- Move a few steps away from your cat and blow the whistle – she should come over to you. If she does, praise her and give her the reward. If she doesn't then don't reward her, but next time start off by going back to blowing the whistle and giving her a reward straight away.

- Once your cat recognises the noise and will follow you a few steps away, you can then start moving to different places, blowing the whistle and praising and rewarding her when she comes.

I STARTED THIS TRICK ON: ....

I COMPLETED THIS TRICK BY: ....

TOUCH AN OBJECT WITH PAW

2–4 WEEKS

TASTY TREATS AND TREAT BOWL, TARGET STICK OR EQUIVALENT

PAW

This is a great trick for when you want your cat to engage with an object. You need to start off with a target stick but once your cat is confidently doing it you can transfer to any object, including a keyboard. My favourite memory of teaching this trick was to a seal-point Persian called Storm – it was for a Cravendale milk advert, and I had to make her look as if she was embroidering! This is a fairly easy trick for your cat to learn, as they are naturally inquisitive with their paws.

I'd recommend using a target stick, which you can buy from a pet shop – with dogs I use my hands at first, but as cats have sharp claws that can hurt! If you don't want to buy a target stick you can use a homemade version, such as a table-tennis ball taped to the bottom of an empty wrapping paper roll or stick.

HOW TO START

Kneel in front of your cat with the target stick.

HOW TO DO

- First, ask your cat to give you his paw.

- Then introduce the target stick by stroking the front of his paw with the end of the target stick and saying '**paw**'. This should cause him to lift his paw. As soon as he does this tell him 'good' and reward him with a treat. Keep doing this until he lifts his paw every time you ask.

- Now you can start introducing the cue '**touch**'. Place the target stick in front of him within reaching distance, rather than touching his paw. Ask him to '**touch**'. Praise and reward him. If he doesn't touch the stick, try and take the stick towards his paw and encourage him to touch it. You can even touch his paw with the target and reward that initially.

- Once he is reliably touching the target stick when you ask then you can start introducing other objects, such as a can. Place it in front of him within reaching distance. Use the target stick and the cue '**touch**' to guide his paw until it is touching the object, then praise and reward.

- After a session or two like this remove the target stick and just use your hand pointing to the object and the word **touch** as the cues.

- You can then change the object again, using something even more fun, like a keyboard!

I STARTED THIS TRICK ON: ....

I COMPLETED THIS TRICK BY: ....

NUDGE

4–6 WEEKS

TASTY TREATS AND TREAT
BOWL, A SMALL PLASTIC
BOWL OR CUP

—

This is similar to the previous trick, but this time the contact should be with your cat's nose rather than paw – which means you can eventually teach her to move an object (if it's very light) over a small distance. It's quite an easy one to teach, but that varies depending on how nudge-y or rubby your cat is naturally.

HOW TO START

You need a small plastic bowl or cup that is light enough for your cat to move and that you can place a treat underneath without the object falling over. Sit in front of your cat.

HOW TO DO

- Place the object in front of your cat and then show her you are putting a treat underneath it. Say '**nudge**'. Hopefully she will nudge at the cup to get the treat. If she does then say 'good' and uncover the treat straight away by tilting the cup or bowl away from her so she can get it.

- Do this again, hopefully building the strength of the nudge as you go. If your cat uses her feet at all make sure she doesn't get the treat this way, only for nudging with her nose.

- Once you feel your cat is really understanding the trick then you can stop putting the treat under the cup and just ask her to nudge it – and then you can reward her with a treat afterwards. You can then swap in any object, so long as it's light enough for your cat to move.

TIP

If she's finding nudging the object over too difficult, then balance the edge of the cup or bowl on a pen or something similar to make it easier for her – this will also keep her enthusiasm up and stop her getting frustrated.

I STARTED THIS TRICK ON: ....

I COMPLETED THIS TRICK BY: ....

JUMP THROUGH HOOP

2–3 WEEKS

TASTY TREATS AND TREAT
BOWL, PLASTIC HOOP

—

*This is quite an easy one to teach – I use it in
training as it's fun for the cats (and me!) to do.
This is an active trick so I wouldn't advise
doing it with older cats.*

HOW TO START

You'll need a big plastic hoop – like the ones children hula with. Position your cat in front of you.

HOW TO DO

- Hold the plastic hoop upright, with the edge touching the ground to start with. With a treat, lure him through the hoop whilst saying '**jump**'. Once he is completely through the hoop, praise and reward him with the treat.

- In the beginning your cat will just be walking through the hoop to get the idea, but as he gets quicker start to raise the hoop slightly so that he has to do a little hop to get through.

- Once he is hopping through the hoop consistently, you can stop using the treat as a lure and just use the hoop and the cue, '**jump**'.

- Keep increasing the height of the hoop ever so slightly each time, until your cat has to jump through rather than hop. Make sure you go at your cat's pace, though, as some will progress quicker than others, depending on how active they are.

I STARTED THIS TRICK ON: ....

I COMPLETED THIS TRICK BY: ....

WALK ON BACK LEGS

2–4 WEEKS

TASTY TREATS AND
TREAT BOWL

—

This is another favourite of mine from the Cravendale milk advert – I had to get several cats to walk in to steal the milk! Depending on your cat's natural curiosity, it's fairly easy to teach, but don't do it with older cats as it can put too much strain on the back legs.

HOW TO START

Have your cat standing in front of you and stand facing her.

HOW TO DO

- Pop a treat in your treat bowl. Show it to her then take it up above her head, so that her front paws lift off the ground, whilst saying '**stand up**'. Praise and reward her with the treat – it is important to try and do this whilst she is up, as this will help her learn what you want from her more quickly.

- Keep doing this, raising the bowl a little higher each time until she is properly standing.

- Once she is standing well then you can start to entice her to walk forwards by keeping the bowl at her head height and moving it away from her. Take this trick, quite literally, one step at a time!

If your cat isn't catching on to what you want her to do, then you can use a support, such as a stick. Place it under her front legs and very gently use it to lift her a little way, until she better understands the task. Once she understands – and you're sure she can hold her own weight – you can start taking the support away.

I STARTED THIS TRICK ON: ....

I COMPLETED THIS TRICK BY: ....

JUMP UP

2–3 WEEKS   TASTY TREATS AND TREAT   —
                          BOWL, WHISTLE OR
                          EQUIVALENT, CHAIR

This is quite an easy trick that involves your cat jumping up onto something. I've used this trick in lots of films, but (as with 'lie down') the most memorable was in the James Bond film, Spectre *– I used it to get the cat (a chinchilla Persian called Ace) to jump onto Daniel Craig's lap.*

HOW TO START

Use something like a chair or sofa to teach this trick.
Make sure it is a nice solid chair – nothing too light that
he could knock over or wobble, as this will worry him. As
usual, have a bowl and his favourite treat ready. Place him
in front of the chair.

HOW TO DO

- Show your cat the treat in the bowl and use it as a lure
  to get him up onto his back legs. Try to have him rest
  his front legs on the chair. Tell him 'good' and give him
  the treat.

- When he has done this 4–6 times, start to lure him all
  the way onto the chair. I use the word '**up**'. As soon as
  he jumps up, praise him and give him the treat.

- Place him back onto the floor and do this several times.
  Only give the treat now when your cat has fully jumped
  up. He should start to understand to jump straight up
  onto the chair without hesitating.

- When he is understanding **up** is a full jump up, try other areas around the house. You can then add a person sitting on the chair, and teach your cat to jump onto a lap.

I STARTED THIS TRICK ON: ....

I COMPLETED THIS TRICK BY: ....

STRETCH

4–6 WEEKS

TASTY TREATS AND
TREAT BOWL

STAY

This trick gets your cat to stretch so that her tummy is down and back up. I use this either to make a cat look tired or bored, or you can double it up as a bow. I'd recommend teaching this after dinner when your cat isn't too hungry – otherwise she will cheat lots, as you need to hold the food close to her nose!

HOW TO START

Have your cat in a standing position and have the treat bowl ready in your hand with a treat already in it.

HOW TO DO

- Place your free hand gently under your cat's tummy. Hold the treat in front of her nose and lure her front end down towards the floor. You will need to bring the bowl down and slightly away from her to get the stretch. Tell her to stay as you do this, otherwise she will leap onto the bowl!

- As soon as she goes even slightly into the stretch, tell her 'good' and give her the treat.

- Continue to do this, taking the bowl slightly further back each time to enable her to do a full stretch, adding the cue '**stretch**'.

- Once she has done this reliably quite a few times, remove your supporting hand and tell her to '**stretch**' and stay. If she does the trick correctly then praise and reward her, but she will most likely lie down!

If she does this, gently tap her back at the base of her tail. This often brings up their back end. Reward that straight away. If that doesn't work, go back to putting your hand underneath and try to edge it out slowly, using just fingertips, before removing your hand altogether.

I STARTED THIS TRICK ON: ....

I COMPLETED THIS TRICK BY: ....

PAD

3–5 WEEKS

TASTY TREATS AND TREAT BOWL, COMFY BLANKET (OPTIONAL)

—

This trick gets your cat to place his paws on a surface and 'paddle' it up and down, like kneading bread. It's a trick you can encourage but that cats need to do naturally – you reward the behaviour as soon as they've done it and add in the cue.

Your cat will enjoy this trick a lot! I have used this in the past, combining a stretch (page 69) and pad for an advert for cat litter, to make it look as if the cat was massaging somebody!

HOW TO START

I tend to train this trick on my lap. If your cat doesn't really like sitting on your lap, you can use a thick comfy blanket for him to lie on instead.

HOW TO DO

- With your cat either on your lap or on the blanket, stroke him gently until he relaxes. What you're looking for is for him to move his feet – as soon as he even twitches his paw then praise him and give him a treat.

- Repeat the process again, waiting for him to twitch his foot, and this time when he does it add the cue '**pad**'. Do this three or four times. If your cat is twitching well, wait a little before rewarding him and it should develop into padding. It is good to try and increase the number of times your cat pads with his feet – often once you reward your cat it takes a while to settle them again, as they get excited!

- Keep doing this until your cat really understands what he is being rewarded for, and then you can start just using the cue '**pad**' rather than starting with a stroke on your lap or on the blanket.

TIP

Tickling your cat can often bring about a pad faster.

I STARTED THIS TRICK ON: ....

I COMPLETED THIS TRICK BY: ....

HEAD DOWN

3–5 WEEKS

TASTY TREATS AND
TREAT BOWL

LIE DOWN,
STAY

This is for when you want your cat to lie down and put her head on the floor. I've used this in films to make cats look innocent or sad.

HOW TO START

Ask your cat to lie down, then praise and reward this as you normally would. Have another treat ready.

HOW TO DO

- Once she is lying comfortably, take the treat in one hand and gently touch the top of her head. Reward her for staying in the lying down position and allowing this. I always use baby steps in this trick, to keep the cat calm. Do this several times so your cat is comfortable with you touching her head.

- Next, move on to luring her head down with the treat and (very!) gently pressing on her head so her chin is on the floor. Add the cue '**head down**'. As soon as she lowers her head praise and reward her.

- Keep doing this until you barely have to touch her head, always remembering to praise and reward.

- After that, you should be able to just use the **head down** cue and the hand gesture of lowering the treat to get her to do the trick, rather than you needing to help her.

- Once she is doing this well, try to back away slightly and ask her to '**head down**' without luring with the treat – I tend to point to the floor instead. As soon as her chin hits the floor, rush in to praise and reward her with a treat.

- Once she is reliably doing this every time, you can start increasing the length of time in the head down position by asking her to '**stay**' when her head is on the ground.

I STARTED THIS TRICK ON: ....

I COMPLETED THIS TRICK BY: ....

LIE ON BACK

3–5 WEEKS

TASTY TREATS AND TREAT
BOWL, COMFY BLANKET
OR BED

LIE DOWN,
STAY

*I had to teach this for a Freeview ad which
involved a budgie and a cat falling in love.
The cat and the budgie had to lie down together
– although in real life they never did this at the
same time! The budgie was added in later with
some clever film work.*

*Your cat needs to have a laid-back personality
for this one, and you'll need a comfy surface to
train this on, such as a bed or a nice blanket.*

HOW TO START

Ask your cat to lie down on the blanket or bed and praise and reward him for this as you usually would.

HOW TO DO

- Take a treat towards his shoulder and raise it up and over his body, encouraging him to roll over onto his side. Praise and reward this. Do this until he is comfortable rolling onto his side.

- Then introduce the cue '**over**', and start moving the treat further over your cat so that he moves from his side onto his back. You can try to praise and reward him on his back by letting him turn his head to the side to take the treat, but it's sometimes hard to do this, so often I let him get up for his treat. Lots of cats don't like their tummy being rubbed so it is also easier to pet him once he's up.

- Keep doing this, and then add 'stay' when your cat is on his back, to encourage him to stay in that position.

TIP

If your cat rolls straight over rather than staying on his back you can create a barrier with a cushion.

I STARTED THIS TRICK ON: ....

I COMPLETED THIS TRICK BY: ....

JUMP OVER

2–4 WEEKS

TASTY TREATS AND TREAT
BOWL, BROOM HANDLE
OR EQUIVALENT

—

*This is an active trick (so only do it with young
cats) and one that is easy if your cat is playful.
I had to teach this quite recently with a tabby cat
called Tinkerbelle for a BBC documentary called
Cats v Dogs – it was to show who could jump
higher out of cats and dogs. Cats won by a mile!*

HOW TO START

You need to set up something little for your cat to jump over – just a few inches off the floor. I use a broom handle – you need something low but long. Stand your cat to the side of the jump.

HOW TO DO

- Take the treat in the bowl towards your cat so she sees it. Bring the treat away from her and over the jump so she follows it – try to avoid her going around it by taking the treat over the centre of the jump. As soon as she steps over it say '**jump**' and then praise her and let her have the treat. Do this 3–4 times.

- Once she's doing this comfortably you can start raising the jump. Do this in very small steps to build her confidence – just a few inches at a time – because if you rush she will start running underneath or around it. Keep repeating by luring her over with the treat. Once she is comfortable with each stage, raise the jump slightly higher.

- Eventually you should be able to phase out the luring with the treat, and be able to say '**jump**' before rewarding with a treat at the end.

TIP

If your cat does start running underneath the jump, then go back to a lower height and get her to do that one consistently before you raise it again. Make sure you're not raising the bar too quickly.

I STARTED THIS TRICK ON: ....

I COMPLETED THIS TRICK BY: ....

RUB

2–4 WEEKS

TASTY TREATS AND TREAT BOWL

—

This trick involves your cat rubbing up against you or an object. Like 'pad', this is a trick you can encourage but that needs to occur naturally – when it does you quickly swoop in and reward it! I used this with Blofeld's iconic white fluffy cat in Spectre (called Ace in real life); he had to rub up against Christoph Waltz's legs.

HOW TO START

I train this using myself as the object for the cat to rub against, as it can become too confusing for them to begin with another person or object involved. Stand in front of your cat holding the treat bowl with a treat in it.

HOW TO DO

- Show him you have a treat. He may well sit and wait for you to give it to him. Just stand still and see if he naturally stands up and rubs against your legs. If he does, praise and reward him straight away. Some cats will do this very quickly, as they are natural rubbers! But most cats usually get up eventually to try and nudge you into giving them the treat. As soon as the side of his body touches your leg, praise and reward him.

- Start the process again – this time when your cat rubs or touches your leg with the side of his body say '**rub**' and try to get him to stay for a little longer before you praise and reward him. Cats like the feeling of rubbing, so it should come naturally.

- Once he has learnt this trick on you, you can transfer it onto objects, such as a chair or the couch. Just stand him beside the object, point to it and ask him to **rub**. As soon as he does it praise and reward him with a treat.

TIP

If you have a cat that is not a natural rubber and isn't touching your leg, then try to lure him around the bottom of your legs with the treat. As soon as he moves to your legs praise him and give him the treat.

Do it again, and this time keep the treat very tight to your legs so that he touches them and starts to understand that this is what you are asking him to do. Start luring him around your legs with the treat and praise and reward him when he is back in front of you (i.e. he has done a full circle). Do this quite a few times – when he touches you say '**rub**' before giving him praise and the treat.

The aim is to then stop luring him and see if he just circles your legs when you say '**rub**'. As he circles, if he touches you at any point give him a 'good boy' and the treat. He should make the connection that he should rub/touch you as he goes around.

WAVE

2–4 WEEKS | TASTY TREATS AND TREAT BOWL, TARGET STICK OR EQUIVALENT | SIT, TOUCH WITH PAW, STAY

I love this trick – it's a real crowd pleaser and is always super cute. If your cat knows how to touch something with his paw this will be a quick trick to teach.

HOW TO START

I find this easier to teach with a target stick, which you can buy from a pet shop. If you don't want to buy a target stick you can use a homemade version, such as a table-tennis ball taped to the bottom of an empty wrapping paper roll or stick.

Sit your cat in front of you and have the target stick ready.

HOW TO DO

- Ask her to '**touch**', but have the target stick slightly above her shoulder height and just out of reach. As soon as she raises her paw praise and reward her. I take the target stick back within reach of the cat as I reward – so that her paw is still off the ground. Keep doing this, adding in the cue '**wave**'.

- Build up the length of time her paw is up by adding in a 'stay' as well, so '**wave, stay, wave**'.

TIP

If your cat is a bit wobbly with the touch trick you can gently lift her paw with the target stick. As soon as her paw comes off the ground, reward her. Keep doing this until you just touch her paw with the target stick and she raises it herself without your help. The next step is for her to raise her paw without you touching it. As soon as she does this, say '**wave**' then give her a big 'good'. Try to prolong the time her paw is up before giving her the treat.

I STARTED THIS TRICK ON: ....

I COMPLETED THIS TRICK BY: ....

LIE ON SIDE

4–6 WEEKS   TASTY TREATS AND TREAT BOWL   LIE DOWN

This trick is for when you want your cat to roll onto his side rather than lying flat – sometimes used in film and TV for playing dead. It's quite an advanced trick; your cat will need to be very familiar with 'lie down' (page 41) before you give this a go and they'll also need to feel safe and secure. I used this most recently in Game of Thrones *Season 2: a Maine Coon tabby called Max had to jump onto a bed and lie on his side.*

HOW TO START

Have a treat in your hand, then kneel in front of your cat and ask him to lie down.

HOW TO DO

- Gently place your treat-free hand on your cat's side. Move your hand with the treat in it down to the side, gently coaxing his body to move in that direction whilst saying '**on your side**'. He probably won't turn onto his side immediately, so what you're looking for is his shoulder touching the ground. As soon as that happens praise and reward him.

- Repeat the process, but try to get your cat to go a little more onto his side each time before praising and rewarding him. Keep doing this until he is lying flat out and you no longer need to use your hands as prompts.

TIP

Never force your cat onto his side – you can assist gently, but he won't understand what's expected of him if he doesn't make the decision to lie on his side by himself.

I STARTED THIS TRICK ON: ....

I COMPLETED THIS TRICK BY: ....

ROLL OVER

2–4 WEEKS

TASTY TREATS AND
TREAT BOWL

LIE DOWN,
LIE ON SIDE

This is a very sweet trick where your cat rolls from one side to the other. It can be a little tricky depending on the personality of your cat, but if your cat likes to rub then you'll find this one pretty easy. I'd recommend only doing this trick with a very calm cat, as excitable cats like to swipe at you playfully with their paws whilst they are in this position!

HOW TO START

Kneel facing your cat and ask her to lie on her side. Have a treat in your hand.

HOW TO DO

- Use the treat to draw an arc over her head and down to the side she isn't lying on – as her head follows the treat, her body should too. Use the words '**roll over**' as you do this.

- Keep repeating until your cat is doing this confidently each time. Then you can stop using food as the lure and just use the cue and finger movement to get her to do it.

I STARTED THIS TRICK ON: ....

I COMPLETED THIS TRICK BY: ....

BACK UP

....

3–5 WEEKS

**TASTY TREATS AND TREAT
BOWL, BLOCK OF WOOD/BIG,
HEAVY BOOK**

–

*This is quite an advanced trick, which involves
your cat backing away from you. It's used in
films and TV when the cat needs to look as if
he's getting an actor's attention, or to convey
that he's scared, or perhaps to be sly: I remember
teaching this to Crackerjack (who played
Crookshanks) for this reason.*

HOW TO START

Position your cat in front of an object, such as a block of wood or large book. Kneel in front of him and pop a treat in your hand.

HOW TO DO

- Show your cat the treat and use it as a lure to encourage him to back up by moving the treat slowly past him, backwards, but not so high that he looks up and sits down. As soon as your cat's back feet come into contact with the object, praise him and give him the treat. Repeat several times, introducing the cue **'back up'** when you start luring your cat backwards.

- To start with, the distance between the cat and the object should be tiny. Once he starts connecting with the object more quickly and confidently you can start the trick with the object slightly further away, encouraging your cat to cover more distance when moving backwards.

TIP

Even if you feel he is understanding this, you should still throw in a short back-up every now and then, so he can have an easy win!

I STARTED THIS TRICK ON: ....

I COMPLETED THIS TRICK BY: ....

HOLD OBJECT

6–8 WEEKS

TASTY TREATS AND TREAT
BOWL, A SMALL CAT TOY OF
YOUR CHOICE

—

This is an advanced trick, mainly because while cats will naturally pick things up with their mouths, you a) need them to pick up an object of your choosing and then b) get them to hold it there. But it's very satisfying once they've done it – and then you can move on to 'bring object' (page 107) where the possibilities are endless!

HOW TO START

You need an object that will be light and comfortable for your cat to hold in her mouth, such as a toy mouse (and not something your cat might try and eat or accidentally choke on). Position your cat in front of you.

HOW TO DO

- Present the toy to your cat by putting it close to her mouth before popping it on the floor and asking her to '**pick it up**'. If your cat makes any gesture towards the toy with her mouth then tell her 'good' and reward her. It is important for this exercise only to reward any interest with the mouth and not with the feet, or you might confuse your cat.

- Keep repeating until she actually has the toy in her mouth – make a big fuss of this and reward her with a treat.

- Once your cat is properly picking the toy up regularly, the aim then is to get her to keep hold of it. Once it is in her mouth, say '**hold**' – if she keeps it in her mouth for a second then praise her and give her a treat. Keep repeating and build the time up very slowly – at first

reward for one second, then two seconds, then three, and so on. Do this over several training sessions – always little and often.

TIP

The key to this trick is patience – be aware that it may take quite a few training sessions to get her to put her mouth on the toy. This is an exercise that is very dependent on each individual cat, so try different things to start the process off if it isn't working for you – some cats prefer to take hold of a moving object as you wiggle it a bit, rather than picking it up off the ground.

I STARTED THIS TRICK ON: ....

I COMPLETED THIS TRICK BY: ....

BRING OBJECT

8–10 WEEKS   TASTY TREATS AND TREAT   HOLD OBJECT
BOWL, A SMALL CAT TOY OF
YOUR CHOICE, A BOWL/LARGE
BISCUIT TIN LID

This is a fun trick that involves getting your cat to take an object somewhere. This is an advanced trick – only attempt it if you have lots of patience! But it's completely worth it – I've used this in lots of films, including with Crackerjack (who played Crookshanks) for Harry Potter and the Order of the Phoenix *– he had to run off whilst carrying an 'extendable ear'.*

HOW TO START

For this you need a little toy or object that is light and soft and that your cat is comfortable holding in his mouth (and not something your cat might try and eat or accidentally choke on) – the object you used to teach 'hold object' (page 103) will be ideal. You'll also need a target for your cat, something large enough for your cat to drop the toy onto – a biscuit tin, large bowl or just the biscuit tin lid is perfect.

Your cat needs to be behind the toy, facing you.

HOW TO DO

- Move the toy to get your cat's attention and tell your cat to 'pick it up' and 'hold' – praise and reward as you normally would if you were doing 'hold object'. (If you're having difficulty with this then go back to the 'hold object' trick and repeat the steps until your cat is performing this confidently.)

- To progress to bringing an object, you need to use your target object. It is better to put the target right below your cat initially, rather than having them travel to it.

- Ask your cat to hold the toy. Once you stop saying 'hold' and so your cat drops the toy, introduce the cue **'drop it'**. Catch the toy using the target object. If the object misses the target then don't reward your cat, simply start again – but if the toy in any way touches the target then really praise your cat and give him the reward. Repeat the process.

- Once your cat is dropping the toy into the target reliably on command, start moving the target away from your cat, half a step at a time. If your cat struggles with this then reduce the distance you're moving the target.

- Once your cat is consistently putting the toy on the target (be patient – this may take weeks!) then you can start to put the toy slightly further away. For this trick always start off with the 'hold object' cues, and then show your cat that you have the target object so they understand that you want them to bring the object there.

TIP

When training this I often use steel bowls, as the noise the object makes when hitting the bowl can be a helpful cue in showing the cat what they're aiming for.

I STARTED THIS TRICK ON: ....

I COMPLETED THIS TRICK BY: ....

SUPERSTAR CAT

THIS IS TO CERTIFY THAT:

....

has mastered all the tricks in this book
to the best of his/her ability.

DATE:

....

SIGNED BY:

....

(the 'Facilitating Human')